FREAKY PHENOMENA

THE SENSES

FREAKY PHENOMENA

The Series

FREAKY PHENOMENA

THE SENSES

Don Rauf

**Foreword by Joe Nickell, Senior Research Fellow,
Committee for Skeptical Inquiry**

MASON CREST

Mason Crest
450 Parkway Drive, Suite D Broomall, PA 19008
www.masoncrest.com

Printed in the United States of America

First printing
9 8 7 6 5 4 3 2 1

Series ISBN: 978-1-4222-3772-4
Hardcover ISBN: 978-1-4222-3780-9
ebook ISBN: 978-1-4222-8014-0

Cataloging-in-Publication Data is available on file at the Library of Congress.

Developed and Produced by Print Matters Productions, Inc. (www.printmattersinc.com)
Cover and Interior Design by: Bill Madrid, Madrid Design
Composition by Carling Design

Picture credits: 9, milehightraveler/iStock; 10, Everett Collection/Shutterstock; 12, irisphoto1/ Shutterstock; 13, Anthony Mooney/Shutterstock; 15, RapidEye/iStock; 18, Everett Historical/Shutterstock; 20, KK Tan/Shutterstock; 23, Alexandru Nika/Shutterstock; 24, Marco Saroldi/Shutterstock; 26, GooDween123/Shutterstock; 27, Claudio Divizia/Shutterstock; 28, Kateryna Kon/Shutterstock; 30, Elnur/ Shutterstock; 32, Sean Pavone/Shutterstock; 35, Paravyan Eduard/Shutterstock; 37, Library of Congress; 38, Cecille_Arcurs/iStock; 40, Gearsolid RT/Shutterstock; 41, zoranm/iStock; 43, Nawalescape/Shutterstock

Cover: wildpixel/iStock

CONTENTS

KEY ICONS TO LOOK FOR:

Words to understand: These words with their easy-to-understand definitions will increase the reader's understanding of the text while building vocabulary skills.

Sidebars: This boxed material within the main text allows readers to build knowledge, gain insights, explore possibilities, and broaden their perspectives by weaving together additional information to provide realistic and holistic perspectives.

Educational Videos: Readers can view videos by scanning our QR codes, providing them with additional educational content to supplement the text. Examples include news coverage, moments in history, speeches, iconic sports moments and much more!

Series glossary of key terms: This back-of-the book glossary contains terminology used throughout this series. Words found here increase the reader's ability to read and comprehend higher-level books and articles in this field.

Advice From a Full-Time Professional Investigator of Strange Mysteries

I wish I'd had books like this when I was young. Like other boys and girls, I was intrigued by ghosts, monsters, and other freaky things. I grew up to become a stage magician and private detective, as well as (among other things) a literary and folklore scholar and a forensic-science writer. By 1995, I was using my varied background as the world's only full-time professional investigator of strange mysteries.

As I travel around the world, lured by its enigmas, I avoid both uncritical belief and outright dismissal. I insist mysteries should be *investigated* with the intent of solving them. That requires *critical thinking*, which begins by asking useful questions. I share three such questions here, applied to brief cases from my own files:

Is a particular story really true?

Consider Louisiana's Myrtles Plantation, supposedly haunted by the ghost of a murderous slave, Chloe. We are told that, as revenge against a cruel master, she poisoned three members of his family. Phenomena that ghost hunters attributed to her spirit included a mysteriously swinging door and unexplained banging noises.

The Discovery TV Channel arranged for me to spend a night there alone. I learned from the local historical society that Chloe never existed and her three alleged victims actually died in a yellow fever epidemic. I prowled the house, discovering that the spooky door was simply hung off center, and that banging noises were easily explained by a loose shutter.

Does a claim involve unnecessary assumptions?

In Flatwoods, WV, in 1952, some boys saw a fiery UFO streak across the evening sky and apparently land on a hill. They went looking for it, joined by others. A flashlight soon revealed a tall creature with shining eyes and a face shaped like the ace of spades. Suddenly, it swooped at them with "terrible claws," making a high-pitched hissing sound. The witnesses fled for their lives.

Half a century later, I talked with elderly residents, examined old newspaper accounts, and did other research. I learned the UFO had been a meteor. Descriptions of the creature almost perfectly matched a barn owl—seemingly tall because it had perched on a tree limb. In contrast, numerous incredible assumptions would be required to argue for a flying saucer and an alien being.

Is the proof as great as the claim?

A Canadian woman sometimes exhibited the crucifixion wounds of Jesus—allegedly produced supernaturally. In 2002, I watched blood stream from her hands and feet and from tiny scalp wounds like those from a crown of thorns.

However, because her wounds were already bleeding, they could have been self-inflicted. The lance wound that pierced Jesus' side was absent, and the supposed nail wounds did not pass through the hands and feet, being only on one side of each. Getting a closer look, I saw that one hand wound was only a small slit, not a large puncture wound. Therefore, this extraordinary claim lacked the extraordinary proof required.

These three questions should prove helpful in approaching claims and tales in Freaky Phenomena. I view the progress of science as a continuing series of solved mysteries. Perhaps you too might consider a career as a science detective. You can get started right here.

Joe Nickell
Senior Research Fellow, Committee for Skeptical Inquiry
Amherst, NY

MORE THAN MEETS THE EYE

W e all take in the world through our senses—smell, taste, touch, hearing, vision. The senses often work together with each other, and sometimes sense can trick another. For example, in grade school you may have tried experiment where you put on a blindfold, and someone holds an onion under your nose w you bite into an apple. When you can't see the apple and can only smell the onion, your ser may fool you so you think you're eating an onion.

In a similar way, sight and sound are intertwined. Consider the *McGurk effect*. This percep phenomenon demonstrates how the visual information from seeing a person speak changes way one hears sound. A clip on YouTube illustrates the McGurk effect: an individual repeate says "bah, bah, bah" over and over again. The sound matches his lip formations. Then the p senter tries an experiment—he keeps the audio track the same but shows the man moving lips as if he were saying "fah, fah, fah" repeatedly instead of "bah, bah, bah." When you watch video, your mind plays a trick on you. You hear "fah, fah, fah." It's not being said at all, but beca it looks that way, you hear it that way. The second you close your eyes, however, the "bah, bahs" return.

We often take our senses for granted, but they are re-markable tools. This volume shows how senses can some-times seem to be cross-wired in certain individuals to pro-duce sensations that are outside the realm of the normal. Numbers may have distinctive colors. Sounds can have specific tastes. Senses can also be heightened, approaching

See the McGurk effect for yourself

superhero levels. An American from California, Daniel Kish, for example, is blind, but he can ride down crowded streets on a bicycle using a type of *echolocation*. Bats use echolocation to fly in the dark. They make noises that send out sound waves that hit objects and create echoes, signaling to the bats where the objects are. Daniel has a similar ability. He clicks his tongue and takes audio cues for the sounds that bounce back to him. It's an extraordinary ability that demonstrates that seeing, hearing, touching, tasting, and smelling may go far beyond ordinary expectations.

This volume also looks at the freaky phenomena of amazing memory, fire-walking, and aphrodisiacs.

Bats use sound waves to fly through the dark.

Chapter 1

Synesthesia

The way Lady Gaga was born includes having the capacity to experience synesthesia.

A **linguistics** professor in Taiwan tastes in Technicolor. When Sean Day eats beef he sees a rich blue. Mango sherbet generates a lime green with waves of cherry red in his brain. A bright blob of orange foam appears about four feet in front of him whenever Day eats steamed gingered squid.

Experiencing color when tasting is rare, but this type of extreme connection between the senses does happen. In a 2005 article in *LiveScience*, Ingrid Carey, then a junior at the University of Maine, talked about feeling colors—and that her feelings would produce colors in her mind as well. Confusion was orange and powerful was red. Another individual described feeling the months of the year as a flat ribbon that surrounded her body, and each month generated a color in her perception. February, for example, was pale green.

These people have a unique sensory condition called *synesthesia*, where the senses seem to get cross-wired. Senses that should remain separate intermingle in a unique way. The word comes from the Greek meaning "to perceive together" and "joined sensation." Some synesthetes are like Day and see color when they eat. Others see numbers and letters as having a distinct color. In one study on the condition, a subject recounted how the number 2 was always bright orange and 5 was inherently green, even if they were printed in black ink on white paper. To him, these numbers simply had those colors.

Words to Understand

Cognition: The mental action or process of acquiring knowledge and understanding through thought, experience, and the senses.

Linguistics: The scientific study of language.

Temporal pole: The most prominent part of the anterior (near the front) end of each hemisphere of the brain.

Seeing numbers or letters as having certain colors is called *grapheme-color synesthesia*. Vladimir Nabokov, the Russian-American author of *Lolita*, was afflicted with the condition. When it came to his own initials, for example, he said that the letter V appeared as a kind of pale, transparent pink and the N was a grayish-yellowish oatmeal color.

In an interview with the BBC in 1962, he said, "Perhaps one in a thousand has that. But I'm told by psychologists that most children have it, that later they lose that aptitude when they are told by stupid parents that it's all nonsense, an A isn't black, a B isn't brown—now don't be absurd."

Strangely enough, Nabokov's wife, Vera, also had the condition—she saw letters in colors, but they were completely different from the hues that Nabokov saw. Their son also was born with synesthesia. Another famous synesthete was the Russian classical composer Alexander Scriabin.

When the doorbell rings, a synesthete may see blue spots. This form of the condition is called *chromesthesia*. Music may bring on an involuntarily color experience. An E-sharp may cause a person to see chartreuse, for example. The Russian abstract artist Wassily Kandinsky tried to capture a sound-to-color phenomenon in some of his paintings.

Singer-songwriters Pharrell Williams, Kanye West, Lady Gaga, Dev Hynes, and Frank Ocean all say they have had experiences with synesthesia. Williams has noted

The tomb of Vladimir Nabokov in the cemetery at Clarence in Montreux, Switzerland. The Russian-American author saw letters as colors.

Pharrell Williams has described his song "Happy" as yellow and orange.

that his mega-hit "Happy" is yellow, with accents of mustard and sherbet orange.

Synesthesia may also present in a form in which music is seen and felt. Violins may tickle the face and a trumpet may stimulate the back of the neck. With *number-form synesthesia*, an individual envisions numbers automatically in a pattern

Learn more about synesthesia.

that forms a mental map. Numbers appear in exact spatial locations and patterns. This form combines spatial **cognition** with numeric cognition.

Synesthesia is not caused by drugs, stroke, or any other influence—people are born with this neurological phenomenon. It's estimated about 4 percent of the population has some form of synesthesia. Although the condition has been observed in people for about 300 years, it's only been thoroughly researched over the past few decades. When American neurologist Richard Cytowic wrote the book *The Man Who Tasted Shapes* in 1998, he documented hundreds of cases of synesthesia. The condition is most common among highly talented individuals.

The World's on the Tip of His Tongue

While all synesthesia cases are fairly rare, James Wannerton of Blackpool, England, has a story that is more distinct than others—he has the ability to taste sound. It is a form of *lexical-gustatory synesthesia*, in which a flow of tastes can be triggered by conversation. In a history class, if Wannerton heard about Anne Boleyn, he would involuntarily taste pear. His mouth is overcome with distinct flavors at the mention of many British monarchs—a strange connection that helped him recall facts when it came to exam time. Some of his school friends' names brought forth the taste of potatoes and strawberry jam. A date's name gave him the flavor of rhubarb. When he thinks of his dad, it's processed peas. When he thinks of his mother, it's ice cream. Naturally, he vastly prefers his mother.

In an interview with the BBC, Wannerton explained how he associates locations and directions with taste as well. An unexpected flavor can signal that he's made a wrong turn. He was once driving somewhere that always tastes like cake to him, but when he suddenly tasted ham, he knew he had gone off course and was driving in the wrong direction. Watching TV or a movie can be very unpleasant because the constant stream of noises can trigger a barrage of reactions. Growing up, Wannerton, his parents, and his doctor did not understand his strange affliction. In

Big Troubles from Little Noises

Misphonia, or selective sound sensitivity syndrome, is related to synesthesia. The word literally translates to "hatred of sound." Sound affects your brain and triggers responses in the body. With this ailment, the noises of someone chewing, yawning, eating, or breathing may produce feelings of anxiety, discomfort, disgust, rage, or fear. The negative feelings can be aroused by a fidgety motion, like wiggling a foot. Doctors think it might be caused by a misfiring between the auditory cortex and the limbic system. Misphonians may treat the malady with regular exercise, sleep, and stress management, including meditation.

Brain connections explain why some people find sounds unbearable that others tolerate easily.

his interview, he said that it can be particularly bothersome when a word triggers a taste that he cannot identify. The word *expect* did that for a long time and it frustrated him to no end. Although the taste was long ago buried in his childhood memories, he eventually re-encountered it and was relieved. It was the taste of a Marmite crisp.

The Scientific Take: A Weird Wiring of the Mind

Originally, synesthesia was thought to be a form of mental illness, but now it is recognized as a neurological disorder. A synesthete's brain simply isn't wired in the standard manner. As a young adult, James Wannerton had an MRI scan that revealed an unusual connection between the part of his brain that dealt with sound and the part of his brain related to taste. Brain scans of patients with mirror-touch synesthesia have shown that their minds are different from the average person's. On the one hand, they have greater white and gray matter in the right **temporal pole**, a region that is linked to empathy and has more activity when one is thinking about others. But on the other hand, they have less volume in the area of the brain that plays an essential role in separating the self from others. The parts that distinguish self and other are out of whack. Patients may take medication or practice meditation to control potential sensory overload. While synesthetes often live happily with their unique view of the world, some become shut-ins to avoid overstimulation and losing control. Several studies have speculated that we are all born with synesthesia, but cross-sensory brain activity goes away as we age. When you were born, you had far more brain cells than you needed. A period of pruning happens whereby only the connections and brains cells you need to use survive. So Nabokov was right.

Smounds!

Smell and taste work together to allow us to identify flavors. Recently, scientists have discovered that sound and smell can also work together in odor detection. Neurologist Daniel Wesson accidentally discovered the connection in a mouse study. When he clunked his coffee mug on the lab table, he noted a spike in the odor-receiving part of the mouse brain. Wesson and colleagues published their study results in *The Journal of Neuroscience* in 2010, showing that sounds could enhance or suppress smell. They theorized that this combo reaction could be a new type of sense. They nicknamed it *smound*. Although more research is needed, this investigation may prove eventually that some music can literally stink.

I Feel Your Pain

Mirror-touch synesthesia is a related condition whereby a person feels what another person feels. With this type of synesthesia, the visual and tactile sensations become intertwined. If a mirror-touch synesthete sees a person being touched, they feel that touch as well. A woman with the ailment described her mirror-touch synesthesia on the NPR podcast Invisibilia. As a child, when she saw other children being hugged, she felt the warm and pleasant sensation of those hugs. If a classmate fell in the playground and whacked his head, a sharp pain ran through her head. The person with this condition isn't actually feeling a slap when another gets slapped—their mind is translating a visual perception into a feeling.

The condition has also been likened to a heightened state of empathy. These individuals may feel short around short people, graceful around ballerinas, and smart among scientists. They also tend to imitate others.

Joel Salinas, a Harvard neurologist, has the condition and he will often feel what he thinks his patients feel. When he performs a spinal tap, he feels the needle going into his own back. Dr. Salinas has to be careful. When he watched a movie about exorcism, he felt his own head and neck trying to spin around—he struggled for breath and heard his spine cracking.

Although synesthetes face their challenges, Simon Baron-Cohen, a synesthesia researcher at the University of Cambridge, says they wouldn't have it any other way. He said in an article on the American Psychological Association web site: "For them, it feels like that's what normal experience is like. To have that taken away would make them feel like they were being deprived of one sense."

CHAPTER 2

ABSOLUTE PITCH

Wolfgang Amadeus Mozart (1756–1791) had perfect pitch.

Also known as perfect pitch, absolute pitch is a talent that some people have to re-create a note without a reference note. Ask individuals with perfect pitch to sing a C-sharp and they can belt out a C-sharp without being off-key—neither flat nor sharp. They pull it from thin air. At the same time, these uniquely talented people can identify notes when they hear them played on an instrument. Jane Gitschier, who worked as a researcher with the Institute for Human Genetics at the University of California at San Francisco, studied perfect pitch and found that G-sharp is the most difficult note to identify. Research results on the topic have shown that people fall into two categories—they either have perfect pitch and can identify all or most notes, or they don't have a clue what they're hearing.

Overall, less than 1 in 1,000 are estimated to have the gift, and most musicians actually don't possess it. Relative pitch is similar to perfect pitch, if requiring only slightly less ability. Individuals with this talent can identify a note if they have a reference note to start with. Many musicians do have relative pitch. If given an F, for example, they may be able to identify a G that is two octaves higher.

The Scientific Take: A Tonal Talent

Dr. Gitschier has noted that the trait may be genetic as people who have family members with perfect pitch are more likely to have the talent. One theory is that, very early in life, those born into families whose members have absolute pitch would frequently be exposed to pitch as it related to

Words to Understand

Genetics: The study of heredity and the variation of inherited characteristics.

Neuroplasticity: The ability of the brain to form and reorganize synaptic connections, especially in response to learning or experience, or following injury.

Olfactory: Relating to the sense of smell.

People who speak Mandarin and other tonal languages are more likely to have perfect pitch.

the sound of their names. Early musical training can influence the ability as well.

In 1999, an investigation led by Dr. Diana Deutsch, a psychologist at the University of California at San Diego, revealed that speakers of tonal languages—such as Chinese and Vietnamese—are favored when it comes to perfect pitch. These languages are characterized by rising and falling tones. In Mandarin, "ma" can mean horse, mother, hemp, or reproach de-

Learn about a possible genetic basis for perfect pitch.

pending on the tone. Although Japanese is not a tonal language, rates of perfect pitch are high in Japan compared with other countries. The researchers believe that widespread musical training, often through the Suzuki method may be responsible. The results suggest that many more people could have perfect pitch if they were given musical training at an early age. Having perfect pitch may help with musical memory, and those with it may be more adept at playing music.

Extra Advantages
Peter Huang, a pianist and violinist born with absolute pitch, says that his talent allows him to fill a water bottle without looking at it. The bottle makes a tone as it fills and he knows just when to stop. He knows who is pulling up to his house by the pitch of their engine. He can identify numbers being dialed by the tones the buttons make.

Famous People with Perfect Pitch

The 18th-century composer Wolfgang Amadeus Mozart was notorious for his perfect pitch. One account of the prodigy tells how at seven years old he could instantly name the note produced by a bell tolling or a clock striking. Bach, Beethoven, Handel, and Toscanini all possessed perfect pitch. Twentieth-century songwriter and bandleader Hoagy Carmichael related a story that singer Bing Crosby would fall asleep on a train, and snore in perfect pitch with the engine whistle. Legend has it that rock songwriter and guitarist Jimi Hendrix could not afford a tuner, but his spot-on ear allowed him to accurately tune his axe. More currently, Michael Jackson had the gift. And from an early age, Mariah Carey could sing back any song she heard, note for note. Paul Shaffer and Yanni have also included themselves among those with the note-perfect perception.

Golden Ears

A small segment of the population can hear things that ordinary folks cannot. They have super hearing. They can detect the softest sounds or those at ultra-high frequencies. Today, recordings have been made in formats that are considered super-high resolution, but many music fans have trouble distinguishing subtle gradations in sound. According to *Scientific American*, there is mounting evidence that people missing one sense don't just learn to use the other senses better. Their brains adapt to the loss by giving themselves a makeover. If one sense is lost, the areas of the brain normally devoted to handling that sensory information do not go unused—they get rewired and put to work processing other senses. Mary Bates, who covered the subject for *Scientific American,* wrote, "When the brain is deprived of input in one sensory modality, it is capable of reorganizing itself to support and augment other senses, a phenomenon known as cross-modal neuroplasticity."

An Ear That Never Forgets

Most people have heard of photographic visual memory, but that same type of total recall can apply to sound as well. Several music fans can recall a whole song simply by hearing the first note. One man wrote online: "My wife can play the first 0.5 to 1 seconds of a song, and usually in the first beat, I can recite the artist and song, sometimes even the album and year. I always said if there was a contest of this sort, I would be hard to beat." Other gifted individuals can play a piece, sometimes even a long composition, after hearing it once or for just a brief time. Although he is blind and autistic, Derek Paravacini can play almost any song after hearing it just once. He played a concerto at London's Queen Elizabeth Hall and memorized the parts of 45 instruments after hearing it just a few times. A musical prodigy, Paravacini began teaching himself to play piano at age two. Scientists say that people with autism can be very musically talented. Despite having a developmental disability, they may have an instinctive understanding of musical structure, although it's not understood why. There have been several cases that are similar to Paravacini's. A five-year-old blind Korean girl, Yoo Ye-eun; a blind college student from Chile, Yerko Difonis; and the blind American teen who goes by just Kuha'o are all able to play back compositions after just one listen. The renowned Italian conductor Arturo Toscanini also had the gift—he conducted operas from memory after his eyesight became too poor to read the music.

Senses mysteriously compensate: a person who could not recognize faces heard pings that identified people for him.

His Face Rings a Bell

Lidell Simpson is a deaf person who also has face blindness or prosopagnosia. He cannot recognize faces by sight, but when he encounters someone he knows, he says that he will hear a signature "ping" sound when they appear. Even if a person is just within his peripheral vision, the ping will go off in his head. He was once in a crowded museum admiring the art, when a "ping" went off. It took him a minute, but he eventually traced the ping to a friend of his who was speaking to a museum guard. Researchers have labeled phenomenon such as this as a type of neuroplasticity.

CHAPTER 3

PHOTOGRAPHIC MEMORY

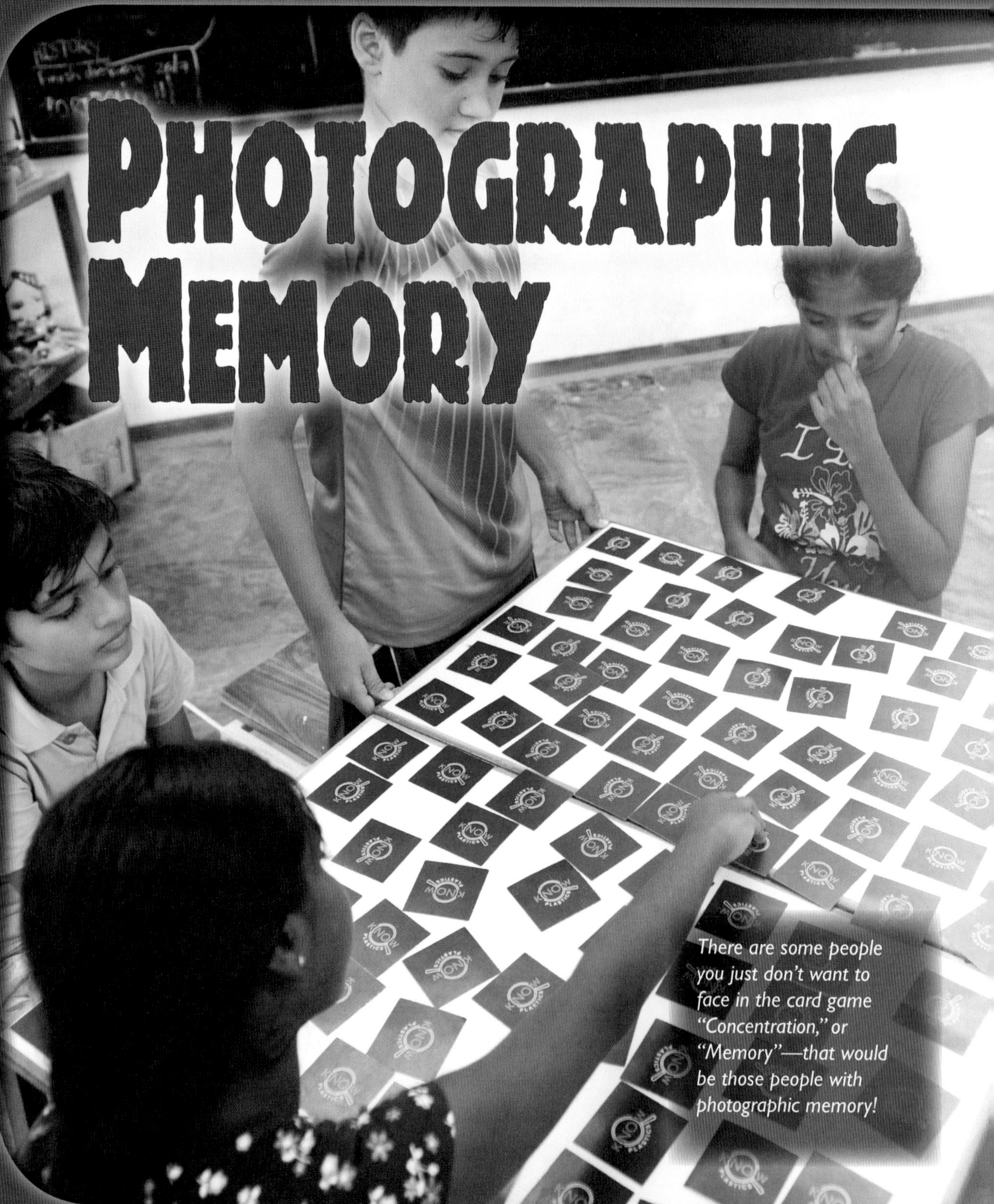

There are some people you just don't want to face in the card game "Concentration," or "Memory"—that would be those people with photographic memory!

Photographic memory, sometimes called *eidetic memory*, is an ability to vividly recall images with high precision after only seeing them briefly. Those who have the most sharpened form of this ability can look at a photograph for minutes or less, and then recall many of the components in the image in great detail. Often, they tell you what they are seeing in their memory as if they are still looking at the image—hence the term *photographic memory*. The image typically stays for a short time and then it's gone. Children are more likely to have the ability. An article in *Psychology Today* reported that 2 to 10 percent of children may have the skill.

Other people have super extraordinary memory that might not be quite photographic but is still uncanny. Allan Nielsen, a college student, recounted in *Slate* magazine that he can see a person for a few minutes and remember their eye color, clothes, jewelry, hair-style, and make-up in great detail. Teddy Roosevelt supposedly could recite entire newspaper pages. The scientist Nikola Tesla could memorize entire books. The activist Abbie Hoffman, director Guillermo del Toro, and actor Mr. T all are known for their remarkable memories. People with these uncanny memories are often called *mnemonists*.

Mnemonic is a word used to describe things that aid the memory. It comes from the Greek for "of memory." A mnemonic device is a tool that helps the memory. For example, those just learning music may remember the notes indicated by the lines on the staff with Every Good Boy Deserves

Words to Understand

Coitus: Sex

Motor functions: Muscle and nerve acts that produce motion. Fine motor functions include writing and tying shoes; gross motor functions are large movements such as walking and kicking.

Resilient: Able to withstand or recover quickly from difficult conditions.

Synapse: A junction between two nerve cells.

Synthesize: To combine a number of things into a coherent whole.

Meet people with amazing memories.

Fudge (indicating the notes E, G, B, D, F). Mnemonists often use the "method of loci" to retain information. Developed by orators of the early Roman Empire, this technique involves visualizing information as being stored in a particular place. Speakers might think of the main points of their presentation being located in part of their house—their introduction is at the front door, the next portion is in the living room, the next in the bathroom, the next in the kitchen, and the conclusion in the basement. Visualizing the information in a particular room can aid the memory. In 1968, psychologist Alexander Luria wrote a now famous account of Solomon Shereshevsky, a Russian journalist with a seemingly unlimited memory. Shereshevsky could recall long lists of items by taking a mental stroll down a familiar street and imagining the items at various locations along the street.

I Am a Camera

Autistic British artist Stephen Wiltshire certainly seems to be one of the small percentage of adults with a photographic memory. After getting a brief look at a city, he can draw remarkably detailed cityscapes from memory. Following a helicopter ride over New York City, he was able to make an exacting recreation in a 20-foot panorama. He listens to music to stay motivated, often Motown, funk, or disco. He has also drawn London, Sydney, Los Angeles, Tokyo, Amsterdam, Venice, Chicago, and San Francisco. As a child he did not speak to other people—he lived mostly in his own world. While he loved to draw, he could barely speak, only making sounds that were unintelligible. It wasn't until age nine that he could really speak. When he found a love for drawing architecture and cities, his career as an artist took off.

No matter how complex a building was he could draw it. At age 10, Stephen drew

Photographic memory was discovered in a London boy who could perfectly draw the city's architectural landmarks, including the Royal Albert Hall, shown above.

what he called a "London Alphabet," a group of drawings from Albert Hall to the London Zoo featuring structures such as the House of Parliament and The Imperial War Museum. Books of his work were published while he was still a child. In 2001, he flew over London and then drew a perfectly scaled representation within three hours. He did the same after taking a 20-minute flight over Hong Kong. All his city re-creations are astonishingly intricate and accurate. In 2006, he was named a Member of the Order of the British Empire, in recognition of his services to the art world. Not surprisingly, Stephen also has perfect pitch. His brain appears to have diverted much of the energy that would have been allocated to engaging with the outer world toward drawing instead. Today, Wiltshire enjoys the life of a successful artist with his own gallery/store and a profitable business selling originals, prints, and books.

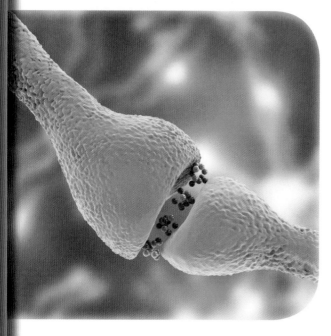

A 3-D illustration of the synapse boundary where essential information passes between neurons.

The Scientific Take: A Compensating Effect

Memories live in the hippocampus and the prefrontal cortex, and for those with incredible memory, these parts of the brain seem to be functioning beyond the normal parameters. There is debate on why this is so. Scientists speculate that autism's effect of delaying language might stimulate eidetic ability. With autistic patients, their brains are not functioning in one way, but then they react by effectively organizing information.

Paul King, computational neuroscientist from the Redwood Center for Theoretical Neuroscience in California, says that memories are stored across thousands of synapses and neurons. He wrote on the web site Quora: "Memory recall is more similar to reconstructing an earlier brain state than retrieving stored data. The recalled memory is never exactly the same as what was stored." He says that the brain is remarkably **resilient**, however. When a person suffers from a stroke, the disruption of blood flow to the brain has the potential to wipe out millions of brain cells in a very short time. But stroke victims have shown that in time they can recover language skills, **motor functions**, and memories, demonstrating that the brain can rewire itself to recover and relearn. Unfortunately, in some cases, as with Alzheimer's disease, memory storage can be permanently damaged. Scientists like King have thought that memories live in the brain's **synapses**. In 2015, researchers from the University of California at Los Angeles discovered that recollections may reside in the brain cells. So exactly how memory functions is still under debate.

Total Recall

Hyperthymestic syndrome or *hyperthymesia* is another incredible type of memory-related ability. The condition is also called exceptional memory or highly superior autobiographical memory (HSAM). Fifty-two-year old Jill Price, an American from Southern California, has been dubbed "the woman who can't forget" because she can remember in vivid detail every day of her life starting from when she was 14.

Give Price a date from any year after she was 14 and she can instantly tell you what day of the week it was, what she did on that day, and any major event that took place—or even minor events—as long as she heard about them on that day. Ask her when the last episode of *Dallas* aired, she instantly knows—May 3, 1991. When did Ronald Reagan die?—the answer is there without hesitation: June 5, 2004. Ask her when was the first time she heard the Rick Springfield song "Jessie's Girl." She has the answer in an instant: March 7, 1981. She was driving in a car with her mother, who was yelling at her. She was 16 years and two months old. When was the third time she drove a car? She says, "January 10, 1981. Saturday. Teen Auto. That's where we used to get our driving lessons from." She was 15 years and two weeks old. On July 18, 1984, she read *Helter Skelter*. On Monday, February 28, 1983, the final episode of *M*A*S*H* aired, and it was raining.

In June 2000, she read about James McGaugh, a neuroscientist at the University of California at Irvine, who specialized in learning and memory. She reached out to him to get a better un-

With the imaging powers of modern medicine, scientists can use brain scans such as computed X-ray tomography to see the brain structures of people with unusual traits, as well as regular patients.

derstanding of her condition. In one of McGaugh's early tests, he asked her without warning to recall what she'd done on every Easter since 1980. In just 10 minutes, she replied: "April 6, 1980: ninth grade, Easter vacation ends. April 19, 1981: 10th grade, new boyfriend, H. April 11, 1982: 11th grade, grandparents visiting for Passover." In an interview with Diane Sawyer on ABC she said, "Every day is a videotape. So if you throw a date out at me, it's as if I pulled a videotape out, put it in a VCR, and just watched the day. As it happened. From my point of view."

Price says this unusual talent can be a curse as well because she can't always control how memories come into her mind—they are not always under her conscious control. They just come pouring in. She wrote in her book *The Woman Who Can't Forget*: "There you are as a 10-year-old in your family room watching *The Brady Bunch*; then you're whisked off to a scene of you at 17 driving around town with your best friends; and before long you're on the beach during a family vacation when you were three. That's how I experience my memories. I never know what I might remember next, and my recall is so vivid and true to life that it's as though I'm actually reliving the days, for good and for bad." Price says that this can be overwhelming—she will relive intense moments of sadness and distress as if they are still happening. She has had to learn to live her life in the present.

Brain scans have now shown that parts of Price's brain are three times the size of those in other women her age and structurally different. Doctors have said that her brain resembles that of someone with obsessive-compulsive disorder. Her greatest hope is that eventually scientists will discover something about her brain that will help solve the disorders of memory loss, a much more common problem about which health care experts hope to gain insight through examining Price's condition. "I've learned from them how many mysteries about memory they're still grappling with, and it does seem that what they've learned about my brain and memory will lead to fruitful research," she wrote.

After McGaugh and his collaborator published Price's story, "A Case of Unusual Autobiographical Remembering," in February 2006 in the neuropsychology journal *Neurocase*, other people with extraordinary memory contacted him. One is Bob Petrella, a standup comic turned writer and TV producer for reality programs such as *The Deadliest Catch*. Marilu Henner, the actress from the sitcom *Taxi*, also has a superhuman memory. Henner gave an example in an interview on CBS: "You say, 'April 3, 1992,' and all of a sudden the whole week starts presenting itself to me. That was a Friday, and I was in New York, actually. Early that week I had won $1,760 at a winner-take-all Academy Awards pool. It was a clean sweep of the Oscars, *Silence of the Lambs*, Jodie Foster." Henner thinks that everyone can improve their memory—all experiences are recorded on the hard drive of the brain and by revisiting experiences and events in your life, you can train your brain, she said.

CHAPTER 4

FIREWALKING

A Shinto ascetic in Nagano, Japan, walks on hot coals. The mystical traditions of the Yamabushi hermits, to which he belongs, go way back.

Strolling across a bed of burning-hot, glowing coals is a scene that has been depicted many times in movies and television shows. In an episode of the TV sitcom *The Office*, the boss Michael takes all the employees to the beach for a day of activities, including a walk over hot coals. When Pam, the secretary, runs across barefoot, she finds it to be an empowering experience. In many cultures throughout history, firewalking has been used in communal ceremonies. There are accounts of the practice going back to 1200 BCE in India. It has been a right-of-passage test for young boys who are crossing into manhood. In the small village of San Pedro Manrique in Spain, the townspeople have celebrated every June 23 for centuries with a firewalking ceremony in which three unmarried women walk across a 23-foot-long passageway of searing embers. Every May in some northern Greek villages, locals celebrate Saint Helen and Saint Constantine with barefoot strolls over sizzling wood coals. They believe that religious power will deliver them over the scorching path without totally roasting their soles.

Watch real firewalking ceremony.

In the modern world, **motivational** speakers, self-help gurus, and life coaches have used the ancient practice to teach individuals about personal growth and how

Words to Understand

Circulation: Blood flow.

Conductor: A material or an object that conducts heat, electricity, light, or sound.

Motivational: Designed to promote a willingness to do or achieve something.

Perspiration: The process of sweating.

Respiration: The action of breathing.

Synchrony: Simultaneous action, development, or occurrence.

to overcome obstacles using mind over matter. The Firewalking Institute of Research and Education in Texas uses the ancient practice to teach people how to overcome challenges in their lives. The institute's founder, Tolly Burkan, claims to have created the world's first firewalking class in 1977, and since that time more than four million people have attended his firewalking sessions. He has given lessons at executive empowerment seminars at Microsoft, American Express, MetLife, and other major corporations.

Over time, he expanded his public seminars to teaching ordinary people how to walk barefooted and unharmed over shards of broken glass. Firewalkers like Burkan think the practice can bring better health and increase personal power. At the basis of the philosophy is a belief in the power of positive thinking. If you harness this power you can create your own reality and do amazing things, even firewalking.

Motivational speaker Tony Robbins used firewalking to inspire people, but in the summer of 2016 at least 30 attendees were treated for minor burns after walking on hot coals during the self-help guru's seminar in Dallas titled "Unleash the Power Within." The fact is, it doesn't always work.

The Scientific Take: Mind over Matter or Not So Hot?

In explaining why firewalkers can cross without burning their feet, scientists have suggested that moisture on the sole of the foot may create a barrier of vapor that protects the soles from harm. The phenomenon is called the *Leidenfrost effect*. It works on the same principle as when an individual licks his finger and quickly touches a hot iron. The moisture on the fingertip creates a protective layer of water vapor. (But don't try this at home!) Scientists say that wood coals are also poor **conductors** of heat. The coals are nearly pure carbon, which is very inefficient at transferring heat. Add to that the fact that ash is a great insulator, keeping the heat in. Also, the events are usually held at night, when coals glow red but under a covering of ash.

You never hear of walking down a path of 500-degree metal, because metal is a great heat conductor and feet would sizzle like hamburgers on a grill. To demonstrate the poor conductivity of wood coals, physicist Bernard Leikind visited the Firewalking Institute—he strapped two steaks to his feet and walked across the coals. The steaks were not at all seared and were barely heated. Also, add in the fact that firewalkers move quickly across the coals, so the feet do not have much time to start charring.

Burkan and others on his staff wanted to prove that successful firewalking is still a question of mind over matter. They walked over a hot metal grill and claimed not to be harmed. The institute maintains that a state of mind is all that's required to overcome the heat. Burkan says that a typical firewalk exposes the flesh to temperatures between 1200 and 1500 degrees Fahrenheit. Those high temps would cause third-degree burns on most people. Dr. Leikind said, "It is my opinion that firewalking is an abnormally dangerous or ultrahazardous activity."

Meticulous preparation of person and place precede the padding over pyres in Sri Lanka.

Research has shown the intimate connection between mind and body. Meditation, for example, can lower the breathing rate, decrease blood pressure, and reduce sweating. Burkan upholds the notion that the mind can influence **respiration**, **perspiration**, and **circulation** to such a degree that the feet can be safe. As long as a walker remains relaxed enough to maintain strong blood flow (and keeps walking), the feet will not crisp up, he says. "I now counsel prospective firewalkers to avoid walking on the embers until they take a moment to look inside themselves at all the conflicting inner voices. Some voices will be saying, 'Don't walk!' and others will be saying 'Walk!' I tell people to first listen to each inner voice, then pay attention to the state of your body. Which decision makes your body more comfortable? If the decision to walk makes you feel more comfortable than the decision not to walk, then walk. Because if you are relaxed with your decision, you are in a certain biochemical state. Whether the relaxation with the decision to walk is based on a belief in physics or a belief in a higher power, it matters not. Both beliefs create the exact same physiology in the body. Unless their bodies are comfortable with the decision to cross the coals, I suggest people wait for another time."

A Unique Mental Boost

When someone is relaxed, comfortable, and confident they are more likely to succeed at firewalking. Burkan says that firewalking shows the potential of the mind to achieve almost anything, and that's why athletes, executives, salespeople, and students have taken a great interest in the practice. Health care providers also see the potential of mind over matter to help with severe illness.

In *National Geographic*, Loring Danforth, an anthropologist at Bates College in Lewiston, ME, said, "[Firewalking] can have the power to affirm one's life. It can change lives, give confidence, all kinds of things."

Ivana Konvalinka, while a bioengineering doctoral student at Aarhus University in Denmark, wanted to measure the physical effects within firewalkers. She noted that successful firewalkers may experience a euphoria, and perhaps their bodies were producing oxytocin, a hormone related to pleasure. In an interesting related finding, the heart rates of relatives and friends of the firewalkers followed an almost identical pattern to the firewalkers' rates, spiking and dropping

A stereograph from 1905 shows men with long pole arranging a pit of white-hot stones in a pit for a firewalking act, as spectators watch from above in the Fiji Islands.

almost in **synchrony**. The heart rates of visiting spectators did not. In an article in *The New York Times*, Michael Richardson, an assistant professor of psychology at the University of Cincinnati, said, "It shows that being connected to someone is not just in the mind. There are these fundamental physiological behavioral moments that are occurring continuously with other people that we're not aware of." Basically, the syncronicity is sympathy, but nothing indicated that this sympathy helped the firewalkers withstand the heat.

CHAPTER 5

APHRODISIACS

It takes more than special foods to get a couple together; but it doesn't hurt.

Nowadays, Viagra may be thought of as an aphrodisiac because it enhances performance when it comes to **amorous** adventures. Researchers at the University of Wisconsin-Madison have observed that the amount of oxytocin released by the pituitary gland increases in Viagra users. Oxytocin has been dubbed the love hormone or cuddle chemical and has been linked to stimulating the libido. In general, however, Viagra has not been regarded as a true aphrodisiac—it doesn't necessarily put you in the mood for love.

Aphrodisiacs are food, drink, or drugs that stimulate sexual desire, and they have been around for thousands of years. The Mediterranean plant mandrake is mentioned in the Bible as an aphrodisiac and natural **fertility** drug. Arabs call it the Madmen's Apple for the plant's ability to invigorate and stimulate the senses even to the point of mental imbalance. (The power of mandrake root is indicated in legends that tell how the plant would scream when it was pulled from the ground—a concept depicted in the Harry Potter novels.)

Throughout time, grapes have also been linked to love, which makes sense since they are used to make wine and can be slightly fermented. In fact, people say alcohol itself is a love potion because it lowers **inhibitions**. The birth rate in the world would probably be a lot lower if everyone refrained from drinking alcohol. The ancient Hindu text of sexual behavior, the *Kama Sutra*, refers to honey to stimulate sexual appetites. Many love potions have featured spices such as basil, mint, cinnamon, cardamom, fenugreek, ginger, pepper, saffron, and vanilla. The ancient Greek and Romans believed that suck-

Words to Understand

Amorous: Showing, feeling, or relating to sexual desire.

Euphoric: Characterized by or feeling intense excitement and happiness.

Fertility: The ability to conceive children.

Inhibition: A feeling that makes one self-conscious and unable to act in a relaxed and natural way.

Oysters have a long history as an appetizer to romance.

ing on anise seeds lifted levels of desire.

When it comes to foods, oysters have long been linked to lust. Casanova, the renowned Italian seducer from the 18th century, was notorious for offering young women raw oysters. He thought they would make him very potent as well, so he sometimes ate 50 for breakfast. His diet apparently worked—he boasted that he coaxed 122 women to be intimate with him. Along those lines, Cleopatra, a ruler of Egypt in ancient times, was said to win the heart of the Roman general Marc Antony by melting down a pearl and drinking it, to entrance him through the pearl's love-enhancing properties. She is also rumored to have rubbed her privates with an almond-honey mixture to drive him wild. King Louis XV's mistress Madame du Barry drove the king mad with passion by feeding him a ginger custard.

Some say the greatest aphrodisiac of them all, however, is not a physical product of any kind—it is the imagination.

The Most Infamous Aphrodisiac: Spanish Fly

For decades, a sexual enhancement formula called Spanish fly was advertised in the back of music and men's magazines, especially from the 1950s through the 1980s. Also called cantharides, Spanish fly gained an almost mythic reputation as an aphrodisiac. Made from crushed, dried carcasses of a green blister beetle found in Southern Europe, the powder has helped those seeking amorous adventures for centuries. It was like the Viagra of the time. The ancient Greek physician

Hippocrates wrote of its powers as did people in ancient Chinese cultures. Reportedly, King Henry IV and the Marquis de Sade relied on it. The treatment should have come with a warning of its potentially long-lasting effects. In the 1800s, a troop of French soldiers who had feasted on frogs that had eaten these special beetles found themselves "standing at attention" for hours. The health side effects can be serious and include a high risk for infection, painful urination, liver and kidney damage, and even death if taken in great quantities.

Explore the fascinating history of aphrodisiacs.

Scents and Sex Ability

You've probably heard the expression "love is in the air." In many ways, the phrase is true because human beings and other animals are attracted to each other through smell. As mammals,

A lot can go right when selecting perfume.

humans secrete airborne chemicals called *pheromones* that send signals about moods, desire, and compatibility. These chemosignals can send different messages ranging from hostility to romance. Perfumes and colognes are designed to create odors that attract sexual mates and activate desire. Some attempt to mimic pheromones. The pheromones are detected in the nose by a region called the vomeronasal organ, which then sends signals that stimulate the hypothalamus in the cortex of the brain. The hypothalamus controls the release of hormones.

Over the centuries, perfume manufacturers have discovered alluring scents from some strange sources. For example, whale vomit contains a flammable, waxy, foul-smelling substance called ambergris, which has been thought of as an aphrodisiac and used to create perfumes. One scientific investigation did find that a chemical in *ambergris* sparked rats into having sex more often. Other popular perfumes include secretions from the anal glands of the civet cat, and *castoreum*, a secretion from the genital scent sacs of the castor beaver.

The Smell and Taste Treatment and Research Foundation in Chicago has discovered that some of the most arousing perfumes attempt to duplicate food odors. Among the most arousing smells are pumpkin pie, licorice, vanilla, doughnuts, oriental spice, and cola. In the non-food category: lavender. Men were especially sexually stimulated by the smell of pizza and women responded best to the scent of Good & Plenty candy combined with cucumber. Although we have yet to see any men's cologne based on pizza, some women's beauty products do rely on a base scent of licorice and cucumbers.

The Scientific Take: Some Work; Some Don't

The effect of aphrodisiacs can depend on the person. Different things make people excited. A person may think dry toast is a turn-on because that's the way he or she is wired. Some say aphrodisiacs are all in the head—like the placebo effect. If you believe it will work, then it works. Although chocolate has been used as an aphrodisiac, the food does not contain ingredients that promote sexual hormones. It may, however, raise levels of serotonin, a chemical in the body that helps reduce depression and anxiety. Also, chocolate contains phenylethylamine, the brain chemical that brings on a **euphoric** sensation.

Scientists have shown that some food, drink, and medication actually do trigger sexual hormones. Take oysters, for instance. In 2005, a team of American and Italian investigators discovered that bivalve mollusks, which include oysters, are rich in amino acids that can raise the level of sexual hormones. Oysters are also high in zinc, which is important for semen production and sexual function. A few studies have shown that the herb ginseng and maca, a root vegetable that has been called Peruvian ginseng, may boost libido and help with erectile dysfunction.

Chocolates are customary Valentines, but they do not promote sexual hormones.

Supplements to Boost Sex Drive

Today, the makers of herbal supplements sell products that promise to lift libidos—and many do contain ingredients that may help. Gingko biloba and ginseng are two common herbal libido boosters. Also, arginine, an amino acid found in meats, nuts, eggs, and cheese can increase blood flood to the genitals. Some plain old vitamins have been shown to help as well, including niacin and iron.

Series Glossary

Affliction: Something that causes pain or suffering.

Afterlife: Life after death.

Anthropologist: A professional who studies the origin, development, and behavioral aspects of human beings and their societies, especially primitive societies.

Apparition: A ghost or ghostlike image of a person.

Archaeologist: A person who studies human history and prehistory through the excavation of sites and the analysis of artifacts and other physical remains found.

Automaton: A person who acts in a mechanical, machinelike way as if in trance.

Bipolar disorder: A mental condition marked by alternating periods of elation and depression.

Catatonic: To be in a daze or stupor.

Celestial: Relating to the sky or heavens.

Charlatan: A fraud.

Chronic: Continuing for a long time; used to describe an illness or medical condition generally lasting longer than three months.

Clairvoyant: A person who claims to have a supernatural ability to perceive events in the future or beyond normal sensory contact.

Cognition: The mental action or process of acquiring knowledge and understanding through thought, experience, and the senses.

Déjà vu: A sensation of experiencing something that has happened before when experienced for the first time.

Delirium: A disturbed state of mind characterized by confusion, disordered speech, and hallucinations.

Dementia: A chronic mental condition caused by brain disease or injury and characterized by memory disorders, personality changes, and impaired reasoning.

Dissociative: Related to a breakdown of mental function that normally operates smoothly, such as memory and consciousness. Dissociative identity disorder is a mental Trauma: A deeply distressing or disturbing experience.

Divine: Relating to God or a god.

Ecstatic: A person subject to mystical experiences.

Elation: Great happiness.

Electroencephalogram (EEG): A test that measures and records the electrical activity of the brain.

Endorphins: Hormones secreted within the brain and nervous system that trigger a positive feeling in the body.

ESP (extrasensory perception): An ability to communicate or understand outside of normal sensory capability, such as in telepathy and clairvoyance.

Euphoria: An intense state of happiness; elation.

Hallucinate: To experience a perception of something that seems real but is not actually present.

Immortal: Living forever.

Inhibition: A feeling that makes one self-conscious and unable to act in a relaxed and natural way.

Involuntary: Not subject to a person's control.

Karma: A Buddhist belief that whatever one does comes back—a person's actions can determine his or her reincarnation.

Levitate: To rise in the air by supernatural or magical power.

Malevolent: Evil.

Malignant: Likely to grow and spread in a fast and uncontrolled way that can cause death.

Mayhem: Chaos.

Mesmerize: To hold someone's attention so that he or she notices nothing else.

Mindfulness: A meditation practice for bringing one's attention to the internal and external experiences occurring in the present moment.

Monolith: A giant, single upright block of stone, especially as a monument.

Motivational: Designed to promote a willingness to do or achieve something.

Motor functions: Muscle and nerve acts that produce motion. Fine motor functions include writing and tying shoes; gross motor functions are large movements such as walking and kicking.

Mystics: People who have supernatural knowledge or experiences; they have a supposed insight into spirituality and mysteries transcending ordinary human knowledge.

Necromancy: An ability to summon and control things that are dead.

Neurological: Related to the nervous system or neurology (a branch of medicine concerning diseases and disorders of the nervous system).

Neuroplasticity: The ability of the brain to form and reorganize synaptic connections, especially in response to learning or experience, or following injury.

Neuroscientist: One who studies the nervous system

Neurotransmitters: Chemicals released by nerve fibers that transmit signals across a synapse (the gap between nerve cells).

Occult: Of or relating to secret knowledge of supernatural things.

Olfactory: Relating to the sense of smell.

Out-of-body experience: A sensation of being outside one's body, floating above and observing events, often when unconscious or clinically dead.

Papyrus: A material prepared in ancient Egypt from the pithy stem of a water plant, used to make sheets for writing or painting on, rope, sandals, and boats.

Paralysis: An inability to move or act.

Paranoid: Related to a mental condition involving intense anxious or fearful feelings and thoughts often related to persecution, threat, or conspiracy.

Paranormal: Beyond the realm of the normal; outside of commonplace scientific understanding.

Paraphysical: Not part of the physical word; often used in relation to supernatural occurrences.

Parapsychologist: A person who studies paranormal and psychic phenomena.

Parapsychology: Study of paranormal and psychic phenomena considered inexplicable in the world of traditional psychology.

Phobia: Extreme irrational fear.

Physiologist: A person who studies the workings of living systems.

Precognition: Foreknowledge of an event through some sort of ESP.

Premonition: A strong feeling that something is about to happen, especially something unpleasant.

Pseudoscience: Beliefs or practices that may appear scientific, but have not been proven by any scientific method.

Psychiatric: Related to mental illness or its treatment.

Psychic: Of or relating to the mind; often used to describe mental powers that science cannot explain.

Psychokinesis: The ability to move or manipulate objects using the mind alone.

Psychological: Related to the mental and emotional state of a person.

PTSD: Post-traumatic stress disorder is a mental health condition triggered by a terrifying event.

Repository: A place, receptacle, or structure where things are stored.

Resilient: Able to withstand or recover quickly from difficult conditions.

Resonate: To affect or appeal to someone in a personal or emotional way.

Schizophrenia: A severe mental disorder characterized by an abnormal grasp of reality; symptoms can include hallucinations and delusions.

Skeptic: A person who questions or doubts particular things.

Spectral: Ghostly.

Spiritualism: A religious movement that believes the spirits of the dead can communicate with the living.

Stimulus: Something that causes a reaction.

Subconscious: The part of the mind that we are not aware of but that influences our thoughts, feelings, and behaviors.

Sumerians: An ancient civilization/people (5400–1750 BCE) in the region known as Mesopotamia (modern day Iraq and Kuwait).

Synapse: A junction between two nerve cells.

Synthesize: To combine a number of things into a coherent whole.

Telekinesis: Another term for psychokinesis. The ability to move or manipulate objects using the mind alone.

Telepathy: Communication between people using the mind alone and none of the five senses.

Uncanny: Strange or mysterious.

Further Resources

Websites

American Synesthesia Association: *http://www.synesthesia.info/*
This association provides information to synesthetes and to further research into the area of synesthesia.

UK Synaesthesia Association: *http://www.uksynaesthesia.com/*
This group brings together researchers and subjects in an environment where they can freely swap information about synesthesia.

Firewalking Institute of Research and Education: *http://www.firewalking.com/*
The institute is committed to personal empowerment and group bonding through firewalking and other programs.

American Herbalists Guild: *http://www.americanherbalistsguild.com/*
The guild provides educational resources regarding herbal remedies.

The Picower Institute for Learning and Memory, Massachusetts Institute of Technology: *https://picower.mit.edu/*
A community of scientists dedicated to brain research, including topics concerning memory.

Movies

Here are a few movies related to some of the topics in this book.

The Soloist (2009)
The movie features an on-screen depiction of the subject of the film experiencing synethesia. This occurs while listening to a rehearsal of the Los Angeles Philharmonic.

Temple Grandin (2010)
Clare Danes plays an autistic woman with a photographic memory who becomes an expert in animal husbandry.

The Man Who Walks on Fire (1986)
A documentary about Hugh Bromily, a master firewalker and British martial artist.

Further Reading

Burkan, Tolly and Andrew Weil. *Extreme Spirituality: Radical Approaches to Awakening.* San Francisco: Council Oaks Books, 2004.

Cytowic, Richard and David Eagleman. *Wednesday Is Indigo Blue: Discovering the Brain of Synesthesia.* Cambridge, MA: MIT Press, 2011.

Dell, Linda. *Aphrodisiacs: An A-Z.* New York: Skyhorse Publishing, 2015.

Duffy, Patricia Lynne. *Blue Cats and Chartreuse Kittens: How Synesthetes Color Their Worlds.* New York: Times Books, 2001.

Harris, Marie. *The Girl Who Heard Colors.* New York: Nancy Paulsen Books, 2013.

Lee, Larry E. and Joe Carroll. *Virtual Memory for Humans: How to Develop Photographic Memory.* Romeoville, IL: Triad Group, 2001.

Perlmutter, Adam. Hal Leonard *Perfect Pitch Method: A Musician's Guide to Recognizing Pitches by Ear,* Book/3-CD Pack with Online Audio. Winona, MN: Hal Leonard, 2014.

Stark, Raymond. *The Book of Aphrodisiacs.* New York: Stein & Day, 1982.

Sternfield, Jonathan. *The Psychology of Physical Immunity.* Great Barrington, MA: Berkshire House Publishers, 1992.

Wiltshire, Stephen. *Floating Cities.* London: Michael Joseph, 1991.

About the Author

Don Rauf has written more than 30 nonfiction books, including *Killer Lipstick and Other Spy Gadgets, Simple Rules for Card Games, Psychology of Serial Killers: Historical Serial Killers, The French and Indian War, The Rise and Fall of the Ottoman Empire,* and *George Washington's Farewell Address.* He has contributed to the books *Weird Canada* and *American Inventions.* He lives in Seattle with his wife, Monique, and son, Leo.

Index